THE TAO OF THE
SPIRITUAL WARRIOR

Daily Thoughts for the
Martial Artist Within Us

Anthony Pillage

THE TAO OF THE
SPIRITUAL WARRIOR

WOTSW Media
75 Dickens Road
Coventry
West Midlands, UK
CV6 2JQ

www.wayofthespiritualwarrior.co.uk
www.anthonypillage.co.uk

ISBN: 978-0-9556838-0-0

Printed in the US

Sponsors

www.woma.tv

www.senishow.com

www.martialartstandards.org

Introduction

I remember with absolute clarity the moment many years ago, that I first felt moved by the power of words.

One sentence in the film *Dead Poets Society* about "*Carpe Diem*" and "seizing the day" and the course of my life changed in a heartbeat. This started a lifelong journey to find that which inspires and changes the perceptions of my existence.
They have been found in all sorts of unexpected places from film to The Bible, from philosopher to child, from martial artist to president.

Many, as my life has evolved, have changed in meaning and translation but they still hold that mystical quality of transformation.

That is the alchemy of the word and of, I believe, practicing martial arts. I hope that some will inspire and provoke thought amongst the readers and maybe, just maybe, alter the way in which you currently view your world.

Rei,

Anthony Pillage

Acknowledgments

Firstly, to my wonderful wife Sarah, who not only designed the cover, but without whose help, love and support my own journey would never had been made possible.

Secondly, to my Jedi friend and mentor Steve Rowe whose wisdom, patience and belief has carried me through some interesting times. A cross between Yoda, Buddha and Denny Crane! Nuff said....

Thirdly, to Joe Carslake Hanshi who is the epitome of all I would aspire to be as a martial artist. A remarkable man.

Others who get a more than dishonourable mention are Gavin "Walloper" Richardson, my Spiritual Brother (God help the pair of us); The totally inspirational Richard Olpin; "Madog" Ken Culhane my favourite training partner;
Deepak Lodhia, a truly beautiful human being; Neil Pottinger, a firmer friend could not be found; Paul Alderson, a visionary, a champion and the receptacle for my own brand of Pillage humour !
Mick Coup; a true Warrior in every sense of the word;
And lastly, Tigger, for being the only real role model for my life. xx

Spiritual Warriors

I would also like to thank the following: Sensei's Eric and Luke Parry, Charlotte Keen, Craig Allsopp, Paul Sanders and all my students who never cease to amaze, confound and inspire me. And last, but no means least, Steve Strong, a superb martial artist, friend and belief-giver;

I thank you all.

Also to all the remarkable martial artists with whom I have trained over the years. Too many to mention but too few to forget. I thank you for your courtesy and patience, your knowledge and guidance.

And of course to the sages and word bringers that have contributed over the last two thousand years to enlighten, entertain and provoke us all.

I humbly thank you for your insight, your wit and your wisdom.

AP
December 2007

The journey of a thousand miles
begins with one step.

Ancient Chinese Proverb

Life is growth.

If we stop growing, technically and
spiritually, we are as good as dead.

Morihei Ueshiba

They're not that different from you,
are they?

Same haircuts. Full of hormones, just
like you. Invincible, just like you feel.
The world is their oyster. They
believe they're destined for great
things, just like many of you; their
eyes are full of hope, just like you.

Did they wait until it was too late to
make from their lives even one iota
of what they were capable? Because,
you see gentlemen, these boys are
now fertilising daffodils.

But if you listen real close, you can
hear them whisper their legacy to
you.

Go on, lean in.

Listen, you hear it? - - *Carpe* - - hear
it? - - *Carpe, carpe diem.* Seize the
day boys, make your lives
extraordinary.

**John Keating from the film
"Dead Poets Society"**

Peace comes from within.

Do not seek it without.

Buddha

To fight and conquer in all your
battles is not supreme excellence.

Supreme excellence consists in
breaking the enemy's resistance
without fighting.

Sun Tzu

Some men see things as they are and
say why.

I dream of things that never were
and say why not.

John F. Kennedy

Our greatest glory is not in never falling but in rising every time we fall.

Confucius

Being a black belt is a state of mind
and attitude

Rick English

The truth is incontrovertible, malice
may attack it, ignorance may deride
it, but in the end... there it is.

Winston Churchill

When you are content to be simply
yourself and don't compare or
compete, everybody will respect you.

Lao Tzu

There is nothing more difficult... than
to take the lead in the introduction
of a new order of things.

Niccolo Machiavelli

Do not go where the path may lead.

Go where there is no path and leave
a trail.

Ralph Waldo Emerson

Success is more attitude than aptitude.

Anonymous

Motivation is what gets you started.

Habit is what keeps you going.

Jim Ryun

Striving for success without hard work is like trying to harvest where you haven't planted.

David Bly

I have not failed 700 times, I have
not failed once.

I have succeeded in
proving those 700 ways will not
work.

When I have eliminated the ways
that will not work, I will find the way
that will work.

Thomas Edison

The obstacle is the path.

Zen Proverb

If you do not change direction, you
may end up where you are heading.

Lao Tzu

Before enlightenment, chop wood
and carry water.

After enlightenment,
chop wood and carry water.

Ancient Chinese Proverb

Using no way as a way; using no
limitations as a limitation.

Bruce Lee

To know the road ahead, ask those
coming back.

Chinese Proverb

Good character is not formed in a
week or a month.

It is created little by little, day by
day.

Protracted and patient effort is
needed to develop good character.

Anon

Don't hurry.

Remember, it's the second mouse
that gets the cheese.

Anon

For every one hundred men you send us:

Ten should not even be here.

Eighty are nothing but targets.

Nine of them are real fighters.

We are lucky to have them, they the battle make.

Ah, but the one.

One of them is a warrior.

And he will bring the others back.

Heraclitus

Keep me away from the wisdom
which does not cry, the philosophy
which does not laugh and the
greatness which does not bow before
children.

Kahlil Gibran

The art of being wise is the art of
knowing what to overlook.

William James

Great spirits have always found
violent opposition from mediocrities.

The latter cannot understand it when
a man does not thoughtlessly submit
to hereditary prejudices but honestly
and courageously uses his
intelligence.

Albert Einstein

A small body of determined spirits
fired by an unquenchable faith in
their mission can alter the course of
history.

Mohandas Gandhi

Karate is like philosophy.

Everyone has their own opinion.

Who is right?

Who is wrong?

Nobody can say.

Each and everyone must try to attain
their goal and show they have
created something in their lifetimes.

Mitsusuke Hirada.

Pain is weakness leaving the body.

Tom Sobal

First they ignore you, then they laugh
at you, then they fight you, then you
win.

Mohandas Gandhi

To laugh often and much;

to win the respect of intelligent
people and the affection of children;

to earn the appreciation of honest
critics and endure the betrayal of
false friends;

to appreciate beauty, to find the best
in others;

to leave the world a little better;

whether by a healthy child, a garden
patch or a redeemed social condition;

to know even one life has breathed
easier because you have lived.

This is the meaning of success.

Ralph Waldo Emerson

The only rule in Martial Arts is never
kick a women in the testicles!

Ed Parker

A young monk inadvertently insulted a great samurai. Although the monk could not understand what he had done wrong, he immediately apologised. The samurai, being a braggart full of self-pride, rejected the apology and demanded satisfaction, No matter how hard he tried the monk could not dissuade the warrior from his foolish position. Being of a lower caste in society, was obliged to obey the ruffians demands, and agreed to meet him at dawn for a duel to the death. As was the custom, the warrior gave the monk a sword and sent him away to prepare for the battle.

The monk, having no knowledge of swordsman-ship or fighting, was sure he would lose his life, and went the master of the monastery for advice.

"Your mind is too full of fear and thoughts about what will happen," said the priest. "Sit in solitary meditation all night, with the sword raised over your head as if to strike. Close your eyes and meditate only on the sensation of 'cool'. When the blade meets flesh, the sensation is one of thin and cool. Clear your mind completely. Empty it and then fill it with one purpose only; when you feel something cool, strike down with the sword."

Though perplexed at first the monk obeyed his master. Throughout the night he held the sword above his head and closed his eyes. His fear was gone, and he waited to feel the sensation of cool steel.

"Fight coward!" cried the samurai. "Open your eyes and fight!"

The monk made no response. He heard nothing and saw nothing. His only purpose was to make his one strike.

It is said that the samurai, after a long period of intense silence, sheathed his sword, bowed humbly in defeat and walked away.

Do, or do not.

There is no 'try'.

Yoda

Karate is for life, not points.

David Walker

A Karate-ka with a Black Belt is like a
turtle on a fence post.

They sure as hell didn't get there all
by themselves.

Anon

Strive for the sharpness of a hawk;
the agility and suppleness of a cat;
the fierceness of a tiger;
and the gentleness of a baby.

Anon

You miss 100% of the shots you
don't take.

Wayne Gretzky

The key to immortality is first living a
life worth remembering.

Bruce Lee

Be as hard as the world forces you to be.

Be as soft as the world allows you to be.

Chuck Merriman

We don't read and write poetry because it's cute. We read and write poetry because we are members of the human race. And the human race is filled with passion. And medicine, law, business, engineering, these are noble pursuits and necessary to sustain life. But poetry, beauty, romance, love, these are what we stay alive for.

To quote from Whitman, *"O me! O life!... of the questions of these recurring; of the endless trains of the faithless... of cities filled with the foolish; what good amid these, O me, O life?"*

Answer. That you are here - that life exists, and identity; that the powerful play goes on and you may contribute a verse. That the powerful play goes on and you may contribute a verse. What will your verse be?

**John Keating from the film
"Dead Poets Society"**

Each day is a new canvas to paint upon.

Make sure your picture is full of life and happiness, and at the end of the day you don't look at it and wish you had painted something different

Author Unknown

All Martial Artists are beginners.

Some of us have just been beginning longer!

J.R. West

Sticks and stones may break my bones, **but I will really hurt you !**

A black belt is nothing more than a
belt that goes around your waist.

Bruce Lee

I'm smiling.

That should scare you.

T-Shirt Slogan

If you want to be successful, find someone who has achieved the results you want and copy what they do and you'll achieve the same results.

Anthony Robbins

Two men looked out from behind
prison bars.

One saw the mud; the other saw the
stars!

Anon

Iron is full of impurities that weakens
it; through forging, it becomes steel
and is transformed into a razor-sharp
sword.

Human beings develop in the same
fashion.

Morihei Ueshiba

Religion is the sigh of the oppressed creature, the feelings of a heartless world, just as it is the spirit of unspiritual conditions.

It is the opium of the people.

Karl Marx

Now we all have a great need for acceptance, but you must trust that your beliefs are unique, your own, even though others may think them odd or unpopular, even though the herd may go

[*imitating a goat*]

"*That's baaaaad.*" Robert Frost said, "*Two roads diverged in the wood and I, I took the one less traveled by, and that has made all the difference.*"

John Keating from the film "Dead Poets Society"

Mister Rabbit says, "A moment of realisation is worth a thousand prayers."

Taken from the film "Natural Born Killers"

Once upon a time, a woman was picking up firewood.

She came upon a poisonous snake frozen in the snow.

She took the snake home and nursed it back to health.

One day the snake bit her on the cheek.

As she lay dying, she asked the snake, "Why have you done this to me?"

And the snake answered, "Look, bitch, you knew I was a snake."

**Taken from "Natural Born Killers"
..based on an Aesop Fable**

No matter what anybody tells you,
words and ideas can change the
world.

**John Keating from the film
"Dead Poets Society"**

From the Film 'Good Will Hunting':

Sean: Thought about what you said to me the other day, about my painting. Stayed up half the night thinking about it. Something occurred to me... fell into a deep peaceful sleep, and haven't thought about you since. Do you know what occurred to me?

Will: No.

Sean: You're just a kid; you don't have the faintest idea what you're talkin' about.

Will: Why thank you.

Sean: It's all right. You've never been out of Boston.

Will: Nope.

Sean: So if I asked you about art, you'd probably give me the skinny on every art book ever written. Michelangelo, you know a lot about him. Life's work, political aspirations, him and the pope, sexual orientations, the whole works, right? But I'll bet you can't tell me what it smells like in the Sistine Chapel. You've never actually stood there and looked up at that beautiful ceiling; seen that. If I ask you about women, you'd probably give me a syllabus about your personal favorites. You may have even been laid a few times. But you can't tell me what it feels like to wake up next to a woman and feel truly happy. You're a tough kid. And I'd ask you about war, you'd probably throw Shakespeare at me, right, "once more unto the breach dear friends." But you've never been near one. You've never held your best friend's head in your lap; watch him gasp his last breath looking to you for help. I'd ask you about love, you'd probably quote me a sonnet. But you've never looked at a woman and been totally vulnerable. Known someone that could level you with her eyes, feeling like God put an

62

angel on earth just for you. Who could rescue you from the depths of hell? And you wouldn't know what it's like to be her angel, to have that love for her, be there forever, through anything, through cancer. And you wouldn't know about sleeping sitting up in the hospital room for two months, holding her hand, because the doctors could see in your eyes, that the terms "visiting hours" don't apply to you. You don't know about real loss, 'cause it only occurs when you've loved something more than you love yourself. And I doubt you've ever dared to love anybody that much. And look at you... I don't see an intelligent, confident man... I see a cocky, scared shitless kid. But you're a genius Will. No one denies that. No one could possibly understand the depths of you. But you presume to know everything about me because you saw a painting of mine, and you ripped my fucking life apart. You're an orphan right?

[*Will nods*]

Sean: You think I know the first thing about how hard your life has been, how you feel, who you are, because I read Oliver Twist? Does that encapsulate you? Personally... I don't give a shit about all that, because you know what, I can't learn anything from you, I can't read in some fuckin' book. Unless you want to talk about you, who you are. Then I'm fascinated. I'm in. But you don't want to do that do you sport? You're terrified of what you might say. Your move, chief.

A sticking feather up your butt does
not make you a chicken.

Tyler Durden

It's not daily increase, but daily decrease.

Hack away the unessential.

Bruce Lee

Boys, you must strive to find your
own voice.

Because the longer you wait to begin,
the less likely you are to find it at all.

Thoreau said, "Most men lead lives of
quiet desperation."

Don't be resigned to that.

Break out!

**John Keating from the film
"Dead Poets Society"**

All lies and jest.

Still, a man hears what he wants to hear and disregards the rest.

Simon and Garfunkel, *The Boxer*

Nature does not hurry, yet
everything is accomplished.

Lao Tzu

If you enjoy what you do, you'll never work another day in your life.

Confucius

Three things cannot be long hidden:
the sun, the moon, and the truth.
Buddha

There are only two mistakes one can
make along the road to truth; not
going all the way, and not starting.

Buddha

It's not the size of the dog in the fight, but the size of the fight in the dog!

Archie Griffin

Sometimes you're the pigeon, and sometimes you're the statue.

Bernie Bickerstaff
American NBA basketball coach.

The more I practice, the luckier I get.

Gary Player

Keep away from people who try to
belittle your ambitions.

Small people always do that, but the
really great make you feel that you,
too, can become great.

Mark Twain

The Eight Fold Path

(1) RIGHT VIEW: Right view consists of an understanding of the Four Noble Truths: Right view also consists of an understanding of karma: "Beings are the owners of their actions....whatever deeds they do, good or bad, of those they shall be heirs."

(2) RIGHT INTENTION: Right intention consists of the intentions of Renunciation, Good Will (Metta) and Harmlessness. The intention of renunciation means that the pull of desire (craving) is to be resisted and eventually abandoned, because it is the root of suffering. "Turning away from craving becomes the key to happiness, to freedom from the hold of attachment." The intention of good will (metta) involves the development of selfless love for other beings. The intention of harmlessness involves the development of thought guided by compassion, the wish that all beings will be free of suffering.

(3) RIGHT SPEECH: Right speech means abstaining from false speech, slander, harsh or hurtful language, and idle chatter.

(4) RIGHT ACTION: Right action means abstaining from killing other sentient beings (not just human beings), abstaining from stealing, and abstaining from sexual misconduct (sexual relations which are harmful to others).

(5) RIGHT LIVELIHOOD: Right livelihood means earning one's living in a righteous way: legally, honestly, peacefully, and without producing harm and suffering for others.

(6) RIGHT EFFORT: Right effort involves the undertaking of four "great endeavours": (a) to prevent the arising of unwholesome mental states (such as sensual desire, ill will, dullness and drowsiness, restlessness and worry, and doubt), (b) to abandon arisen unwholesome mental states, (c) to arouse wholesome mental states (such as the seven factors of enlightenment: mindfulness, investigation of phenomena, energy, rapture, tranquility, concentration, and equanimity), (d) to maintain arisen wholesome states.

(7) RIGHT MINDFULNESS: "The ultimate truth, the Dhamma, is not something mysterious and remote, but the truth of our own experience...It has to be known by insight...What brings the field of experience into focus and makes it accessible to insight is mindfulness." Right mindfulness is cultivated through the practice of the four foundations of mindfulness: mindful contemplation of the body, feelings, states of mind, and phenomena.

(8) RIGHT CONCENTRATION: Right concentration (one-pointedness of mind) "makes the mind still and steady...opens vast vistas of bliss, serenity and power," and helps us to "generate the insights unveiling the ultimate truth of things." It is developed through meditation on specific objects

77

To be yourself in a world that is constantly trying to make you something else is the greatest accomplishment.

Ralph Waldo Emerson

People are like stained-glass
windows.

They sparkle and shine when the sun
is out, but when the darkness sets in,
their true beauty is revealed only if
there is a light from within.

Elizabeth Kubler Ross

Before I had studied Zen for thirty
years, I saw mountains as
mountains, and waters as waters.

When I arrived at a more intimate
knowledge, I came to the
point where I saw that mountains are
not mountains; and waters are not
waters.

But now that I have got its very
substance I am at rest.

For it's just that I see mountains
once again as mountains, and waters
once again as waters.

Ching-yuan

The body is the tree of
enlightenment, the mind like a clear
mirror stand.

Time and gain wipe it diligently, and
don't let it gather dust.

Shen-Xiu

The mountain does not laugh at the
river because it is lowly, nor does
the river speak ill of the mountain
because it cannot move about.

Everyone has his own characteristics
and gains his own position in life.

Speak ill of others, and it will surely
come back to you.

Source Unknown

Every human being is the author of
his own health or disease.

Buddha

Learn how to learn.

The very first step to learning is to become a completely blank slate.

Some ancients have used the terms "blank sheet of paper," "empty tea cup" or "uncarved stone," but they all mean the same.

The hardest thing for the student when he begins training is to throw away all of his preconceived notions and conclusions.

Training is tough.

Because it is tough, it is a martial art.

From the book:
KODO Ancient Ways
by Kensho Furuya

Martial Arts are like a
Buffet.

Try everything: keep what you like.

Throw the rest away.

Mo Teague

Keep a 'happy button' in the middle
of your chest and don't forget to
press it several times daily to remind
yourself to be happy - happiness is a
habit.

Steve Rowe

That which offers no resistance
cannot be broken.

Jeremiah

If we could see the miracle of a
single flower clearly, our whole life
would change.

Buddha

Failure is the key to success; each
mistake teaches us something.

Morihei Ueshiba

Violence, even well intentioned,
always rebounds upon oneself.

Lao Tzu

I went into the woods because I
wanted to live deliberately.

I wanted to live deep and suck out
all the marrow of life... to put to rout
all that was not life; and not, when I
came to die, discover that I had not
lived.

**John Keating from the film
"Dead Poets Society"**

Knowing others is intelligence;
knowing yourself is true wisdom.

Mastering others is strength;
mastering yourself is true power.

Lao Tzu

There are only 8 principles in the Martial Arts and each one can be summed up in one word; feet, posture, breath, mind, internal, wedge, spiral and power.

If all these are in place, you are strong, break any one in an opponent and they become weak.

Steve Rowe

A good stance and posture reflect a
proper state of mind.

Morihei Ueshiba

He who knows others is wise.

He who knows himself is enlightened.

Lao Tzu

The divine is not something high above us.

It is in heaven, it is in earth, and it is inside us.

Morihei Ueshiba

Man fears what he does not
understand.

Nils A. Amneus

You must be the change you wish to
see in the world.

Mohandas Gandhi

Yesterday's thoughts have created your present.

Today's thoughts are creating your future.

James Newman

Obstacles are those frightful things
you see when you take your eyes off
your goal.

Henry Ford

He who smiles rather than rages is
always the stronger.

Japanese Proverb

Think what you have always thought
and you will get what you have
always gotten.

Various Authors

Whether you believe you can do a
thing or not, you are right.

Henry Ford

Do just once what others say you can't do, and you will never pay attention to their limitations again.

James R. Cook

When everyone thinks alike, no one thinks very much.

Walter Lippmann

If you realize that all things change,
there is nothing you will try to hold
on to.

If you are not afraid of dying, there is
nothing you cannot achieve.

Lao Tzu

All things are possible to him that believeth.

Jesus

The key to growth is the introduction
of higher dimensions of
consciousness into our awareness.

Lao Tzu

Somewhere, something incredible is
waiting to be known.

Carl Sagan

You will find as you look back upon
your life that the moments when you
have truly lived are the moments
when you have done things in the
spirit of love.

Henry Drummond

Sometimes the heart sees what is
invisible to the eye.

H. Jackson Browne, Jr

Don't let life discourage you;
everyone who got where he is had to
start where he was.

Ralph Waldo Emerson

How do you get world peace?

You get world peace through inner peace.

If you've got a world full of people who have inner peace, then you have a peaceful world.

Dr Wayne Dyer

He who knows, does not speak.

He, who speaks, does not know.

Lao Tzu

If you want to do it right - simply
don't do it wrong!

Steve Rowe

You can complain because roses have
thorns or you can rejoice because
thorns have roses.

Ziggy Marley

Most men occasionally stumble over
the truth, but most pick themselves
up and continue as if nothing
happened.

Winston Churchill

The only thing we have to fear is fear itself.

Franklin D. Roosevelt

You either walk on one side of the
street or you walk on the other.

If you walk in the middle you get
SQUISH, just like grape.

Mr. Miage

Life does not consist mainly, or even largely, of facts and happenings.

It consists mainly of the stream of thought that is forever flowing through one's head.

Mark Twain

The greatest discovery of my
generation is that human beings, by
changing the inner attitudes of their
minds, can change the outer aspects
of their lives.

William James

True victory is victory over Self.

Morihei Ueshiba

No pessimist ever discovered the secret of the stars, or sailed to an uncharted land, or opened a new doorway for the human spirit.

Helen Keller

People are always blaming their
circumstances for what they are.

I don't believe in circumstances.

The people who get on in this world
are the people who get up and look
for the circumstances they want,
and, if they can't find them, make
them.

George Bernard Shaw

Safeguarding the rights of others is
the most noble and beautiful end of a
human being.

Kahlil Gibran

Excellence is an art won by training
and habituation.

We do not act rightly because we
have virtue or excellence, but we
rather have those because we have
acted rightly.

We are what we repeatedly do.

Excellence, then, is not an act but a
habit.

Aristotle

Do every act of your life as if it were your last.

Marcus Aurelius

It is one of the most beautiful
compensations of this life that no
man can sincerely try to help another
without helping himself.

Ralph Waldo Emerson

I fear not the man who has practiced 10,000 kicks once, but I fear the man who has practiced one kick 10,000 times.

Bruce Lee

If you think strength is the most important factor in martial arts, you will never become strong.

Kensho Furuya

No problem can withstand the assault
of sustained thinking.

Voltaire

Learn as if you would live forever:
live as if you would die tomorrow.

Mohandas Gandhi

Ask and ye shall receive.

Seek and ye shall find.

Knock and it shall be opened unto you.

Jesus

A man who has attained mastery of an art reveals it in his every action.

Samurai Maxim

The unlived life is not worth examining.

The unexamined life is not worth living.

Socrates

When I stand before God at the end
of my life, I would hope that I would
not have a single bit of talent left and
I could say, "I used everything that
you gave me."

Erma Bombeck

There is nothing good or bad, but thinking makes it so.

Joseph Murphy

We do not see things as they are; we
see them as we are.

The Talmud

What would you attempt to do if you
knew you could not fail?

Robert Schuller

If you want to see the brave, look at those who can forgive.

Bhagavad Gita

To injure an opponent is to injure
yourself.

To control aggression without
inflicting injury is the Art of Peace.

Morihei Ueshiba

You are worth defending.

While an instinct to avoid causing pain is admirable, and the necessity of doing so is ideal, there are times when an attacker is just not going to listen to reason.

Anon

A Chinese Story

One day, his horse ran away, and all the
neighbours gathered in the evening and
said 'that's too bad.'

He said 'maybe.'

Next day, the horse came back and
brought with it seven wild horses. 'Wow!'
they said, 'Aren't you lucky!'

He said 'maybe.'

The next day, his son grappled with one
of these wild horses and tried to break it
in, and he got thrown and broke his leg.
And all the neighbours said 'oh, that's
too bad that your son broke his leg.'

He said, 'maybe.'

The next day, the conscription officers
came around, gathering young men for
the army, and they rejected his son
because he had a broken leg. And the
visitors all came around and said 'Isn't
that great! Your son got out.'

He said, 'maybe.'

You see, you never really know in which
direction progress lies.

Alan Watts

143

If you always put limit on everything
you do, physical or anything else.

It will spread into your work and into
your life.

There are no limits.

There are only plateaus, and you
must not stay there.

If you always put limit, you must go
beyond them.

Bruce Lee

A moment's insight is sometimes
worth a life's experience.

Oliver Wendell Holmes

All of the top achievers I know are
life-long learners... looking for new
skills, insights, and ideas.

If they're not learning, they're not
growing... not moving toward
excellence.

Denis Waitley

I shut my eyes in order to see.

Paul Gauguin

If the doors of perception were cleansed everything would appear to man, as it is, infinite.

William Blake

It is only with the heart that one can
see rightly, what is essential is
invisible to the eye.

Antoine Saint-Exupéry

Know yourself.

Don't accept your dog's admiration as
conclusive evidence that you are
wonderful.

Ann Landers

One sees great things from the valley, only small things from the peak.

G. K. Chesterton

To be a **warrior** is not a simple matter of wishing to be one. It is rather an endless struggle that will go on to the very last moment of our lives. Nobody is born a **warrior**, in exactly the same way that nobody is born an average man. We make ourselves into one or the other

Carlos Castenada

Generosity is not giving me that which
I need more than you do, but it is
giving me that which you need more
than I do.

Kahlil Gibran

Perhaps all the dragons in our lives
are princesses who are only waiting
to see us act, just once, with beauty
and courage.

Perhaps everything that frightens us
is, in its deepest essence, something
helpless that wants our love.

Rainer Maria Rilke

Never be afraid to do something new.

Remember, amateurs built the Ark;
professionals built the Titanic.

Anonymous

We must overcome the notion that
we must be regular... it robs you of
the chance to be extraordinary and
leads you to the mediocre.

Uta Hagen

Mere longevity is a good thing for those who watch Life from the sidelines.

For those who play the game, an hour may be a year; a single day's work an achievement for eternity.

Gabriel Heatter

To know what is right and not do it is
the worst cowardice

Confucius

When two tigers fight; one is certain
to be maimed, and one to die.

Gichin Funakoshi

To reach a great height a person
needs to have great depth.

Anonymous

To thine own self be true, and it must
follow, as the night the day, thou
canst not then be false to any man.

William Shakespeare

Everything has its own place and function.

That applies to people, although many don't seem to realize it, stuck as they are in the wrong job, the wrong marriage, or the wrong house.

When you know and respect your Inner Nature, you know where you belong.

You also know where you don't belong.

Anon

When you discard arrogance,
complexity, and a few other things
that get in the way, sooner or later
you will discover that simple,
childlike, and mysterious secret
known to those of the Uncarved
Block.

Life is Fun.

Benjamin Hoff

There was a man that hated his
footprints and his shadow, so one
day he thought that if he ran fast
enough, his footprints and shadow
would not be able to follow him and
then he never ever had to look at
them again.

He ran and he ran as fast as he
could, but the shadow and the
footprints had no problems keeping
up to him.

And he ran even faster and all of a
sudden he fell dead to the ground.

But if he had been standing still there
hadn't been any footprints and if he
had been resting under a tree his
shadow had been swallowed of the
tree's shadow.

Benjamin Hoff

The ultimate aim of Karate lies not in victory or defeat but in the perfection of the character of its participants.

Gichin Funakoshi

When in doubt, knock 'em out

"Big" Vinny Girolamo - NY Hell's Angels

To be able to look back upon ones life
in satisfaction, is to live twice.

Kahlil Gibran

1-2 out of every 100 students reach
Black Belt and of those only 1 out of
every 1,000 achieves his 2nd Dan.

Masutatsu Oyama

The time to strike is when the
opportunity presents itself.

6th Code of Isshinryu Karatedo

Follow not in the footsteps of the masters, but rather seek what they sought.

Unknown

It is good to have an end to journey toward; but it is the journey that matters in the end.

Ursula K. Le Guin

In the end one only experiences oneself.

Nietzsche

"*Did you have a happy childhood*?" is
a false question.

As a child I did not know what
happiness was, and whether I was
happy or not.

I was too busy being.

Alistair Reid

When hungry, eat your rice; when
tired, close your eyes.

Fools may laugh at me, but wise men
will know what I mean.

Lin Chi

A great man is he who does to lose
his childlike heart.

Mencius

Enlightenment is like the moon
reflected on the water.

The moon does not get wet, nor is
the water broken.

Although its light is wide and great,
the moon is reflected even in a
puddle an inch wide.

The whole moon and the entire sky
are reflected in one dewdrop.

Dogen

Any time you sincerely want to make
a change, the first thing you must do
is to raise your standards.

When people ask me what really
changed my life eight years ago, I
tell them that absolutely the most
important thin was changing what I
demanded of myself.

I wrote down all the things I would
no longer accept in my life, all the
things I would no longer tolerate, and
all the things that I aspired to
becoming.

Anthony Robbins

When the student is ready, the Master appears.

Buddhist proverb

May you live all the days of your life.

Jonathan Swift

He who knows not and knows not he
knows not, He is a fool: Shun him.

He who knows not and knows he
knows not, He is simple: Teach him.

He who knows and knows not he
knows, He is asleep: Awaken him.

He who knows and knows that he
knows, He is wise: Follow him.

Bruce Lee

If you can imagine it, you can achieve it: If you can dream it, you can become it.

William Arthur Ward

Nobody can hurt me without my permission.

Mohandas Gandhi

You are now at a crossroads.

This is your opportunity to make the most important decision you will ever make. Forget your past. Who are you now? Who have you decided you really are now? Don't think about who you have been. Who are you now? Who have you decided to become?

Make this decision consciously.

Make it carefully.

Make it powerfully.

Anthony Robbins

Give a man a fish and you feed him
for a day.

Teach him how to fish and you feed
him for a lifetime.

Lao Tzu

Live with passion!

To effectively communicate, we must realise that we are all different in the way we perceive the world and use this understanding as a guide to our communication with others.

Anthony Robbins

You can have everything in life you want if you'll just help enough other people to get what they want!

Zig Ziglar

Whenever you do a thing, act as if all
the world were watching.

Thomas Jefferson

Dare to risk public criticism.

Mary Kay Ash

We cannot truly face life until we face
the fact that it will be taken away
from us.

Billy Graham

Picture in your mind a sense of
personal destiny.

Wayne Oates

I believe life is constantly testing us for our level of commitment, and life's greatest rewards are reserved for those who demonstrate a never-ending commitment to act until they achieve.

This level of resolve can move mountains, but it must be constant and consistent.

As simplistic as this may sound, it is still the common denominator separating those who live their dreams from those who live in regret.

Anthony Robbins

Life is like a boomerang.

The more good you throw out, the
more you receive in return.

Josh S. Hinds

There is no need to boast of your accomplishments and what you can do.

A great man is known, he needs no introduction.

Anon

With great knowledge comes great
responsibility.

Spiderman !

If you want your life to be a
magnificent story, then begin by
realizing that you are the author and
everyday you have the opportunity to
write a new page

Anon

There comes that mysterious
meeting in life when someone
acknowledges who we are and what
we can be, igniting the circuits of our
highest potential.

Rusty Burkus

And in the end, it's not the years in your life that count.

It's the life in your years.

Abraham Lincoln

What you do speaks so loudly that I
cannot hear what you say

Ralph Waldo Emerson

If you were going to die soon and
had only one phone call to make,
who would you call and what would
you say?

And so why are you waiting?

Nothing great was ever achieved
without enthusiasm.

Ralph Waldo Emerson

The brave do not live forever, but the
timid do not live at all.

Anon

The life given us by nature is short,
but the memory of a life well spent is
eternal.

Cicero

The real glory is being knocked to
your knees and then coming back.

That's real glory.

That's the essence of it.

Vince Lombardi

Desiderata by M.Ehrmann

Go placidly amid the noise and the haste, and remember what peace there may be in silence. As far as possible without surrender be on good terms with all persons. Speak your truth quietly and clearly; and listen to others, even to the dull and the ignorant, they too have their story. Avoid loud and aggressive persons; they are vexations to the spirit. If you compare yourself with others, you may become vain or bitter; for always there will be greater and lesser persons than yourself. Enjoy your achievements as well as your plans. Keep interested in your own career, however humble; it is a real possession in the changing fortunes of time.

Exercise caution in your business affairs, for the world is full of trickery. But let not this blind you to what virtue there is; many persons strive for high ideals, and everywhere life is full of heroism. Be yourself. Especially do not feign affection. Neither be cynical about love; for in the face of all aridity and disenchantment it is as perennial as the grass. Take kindly the counsel of the years, gracefully surrendering the things of youth. Nurture strength of spirit to shield you in sudden misfortune. But do not distress yourself with dark imaginings. Many fears are born of fatigue and loneliness. Beyond a wholesome discipline, be gentle with yourself. You are a child of the universe, no less than the trees and the stars; you have a right to be here. And whether or not it is clear to you, no doubt the universe is unfolding as it should.   Therefore, be at peace with God, whatever you conceive Him to be. And whatever your labours and aspirations in the noisy confusion of life, keep peace in your soul. With all its sham, drudgery and broken dreams; it is still a beautiful world.

Be cheerful.

Billy Connolly's Desiderata

• Tread gently on anyone who looks at you sideways. • Have lots of long lie-ins • Wear sturdy socks, learn to grow out of medium underwear and, if you must lie about your age do it in the other direction; tell people you're 97 and they'll think you look great. • Try to catch a trout and experience the glorious feeling of letting it go and seeing it swim away. • Never eat food that comes in a bucket. • If you don't know how to meditate at least try to spend some time everyday just sitting. • Boo joggers • Don't work out, work in. • Play the banjo • Sleep with someone you like • Eat plenty of liquorice • Try to live in a place you like • Marry someone you like • Try to do a job you like • Never turn down an opportunity to shout 'Fuck them all!' at the top of your voice • Avoid bigots of all descriptions • Let your own bed become to you what the Pole Star was to sailors of old...look forward to it. • Don't wear tight underwear on airplanes • Before you judge a man, walk a mile in his shoes. After that who cares?...he's a mile away and you've got his shoes • Clean your teeth and keep the company of people who will tell you when there's spinach on them • Avoid people who say they know the answer. Keep the company of people who are trying to understand the question • Don't pat animals with sneaky eyes. • If you haven't heard a good rumour by 11am, start one • Send Hieronymus Bosch prints to elderly relatives for Christmas • Don't be talked into wearing a uniform • Salute nobody • Never run with scissors or other pointy objects • Campaign against blue Smarties

Kindness in words creates
confidence.

Kindness in thinking creates
profoundness Kindness in giving
creates love.

Lao-Tzu

The only way to have a friend is to be one.

Ralph Waldo Emerson

IF... by Rudyard Kipling

IF you can keep your head when all about you
Are losing theirs and blaming it on you;

If you can trust yourself when all men doubt you,
But make allowance for their doubting too;

If you can wait and not be tired by waiting,
Or being lied about, don't deal in lies,
Or being hated, don't give way to hating,
And yet don't look too good, nor talk too wise:

If you can dream - and not make dreams your
master;

If you can think - and not make thoughts your aim;
If you can meet with Triumph and Disaster And treat
those two impostors just the same;

If you can bear to hear the truth you've spoken Twisted
by knaves to make a trap for fools, Or watch the things
you gave your life to, broken, And stoop and build 'em
up with worn-out tools:

If you can make one heap of all your winnings And risk
it on one turn of pitch-and-toss, And lose, and start
again at your beginnings And never breathe a word
about your loss;

If you can force your heart and nerve and sinew To
serve your turn long after they are gone, And so hold on
when there is nothing in you Except the Will which says
to them: 'Hold on!'

If you can talk with crowds and keep your virtue, ' Or
walk with Kings - nor lose the common touch;
If neither foes nor loving friends can hurt you;
If all men count with you, but none too much;

If you can fill the unforgiving minute With sixty seconds'
worth of distance run, Yours is the Earth and everything
that's in it,
And - which is more - you'll be a Man, my son!

Life is too short to be small.

Benjamin Disraeli

May you live in interesting times.

**Old Chinese Proverb
And Curse**

Do not resent growing old.

Many are denied the privilege.

Ancient Irish Blessing

Live as if you were living already for
the second time and as if you had
acted the first time as wrongly as you
are about to act now!

Viktor E. Frankl

...if you ever get a second chance in life, you've got to go all the way.

Lance Armstrong

A superior man is modest in his speech, but exceeds in his actions.

Confucius

Given enough time, any man may
master the physical.

With enough knowledge, any man
may become wise.

It is the true warrior who can master
both....and surpass the result.

Tien T'ai

If a man should conquer in battle a thousand and a thousand more, and another should conquer himself, his would be the greater victory, because the greatest of victories is the victory over oneself.

Buddha

I dislike death, however, there are some things I dislike more than death.

Therefore, there are times when I will not avoid danger.

Mencius

Go out everyday and make your life extraordinary.

Anthony Pillage

Thinking is the hardest work there is,
which is why so few engage in it

Henry Ford

When you are content to be simply
yourself and don't compare or
compete, everybody will respect you.

Lao-Tzu

I worshipped dead men for their strength, forgetting I was strong.

Vita Sackville-West

Some Warriors look fierce, but are mild.

Some seem timid, but are vicious.

Look beyond appearances; position yourself for the advantage.

Deng Ming-Dao

The dance of battle is always played
to the same impatient rhythm.

What begins in a surge of violent
motion is always reduced to the
perfectly still.

Sun Tzu

Where do you begin?

Perfect is a good place to start.

We must always focus on improving
things that are already perfect.

J. Viol

The obstacle is the path.

Zen Proverb

Self-respect is the fruit of discipline.

Abraham J. Heschel

Strategy without tactics is the
slowest route to victory.

Tactics without strategy is the noise
before defeat

Sun Tzu

Nothing is so strong as gentleness.

Nothing is so gentle as real strength.

Frances de Sales

Fighting is like Christmas.

It's all in the giving

Mick Coup

Each morning when I open my eyes I say to myself: I, not events, have the power to make me happy or unhappy today.

I can choose which it shall be.

Yesterday is dead, tomorrow hasn't arrived yet.

I have just one day, today, and I'm going to be happy in it

Groucho Marx

He Who Knows Others Is Wise.

He Who Knows Himself Is
Enlightened.

Tao Te Ching

Without Knowledge, Skill cannot be focused.

Without Skill, Strength cannot be brought to bear.

Without Strength, Knowledge may not be applied.

Alexander the Great's Chief Physician

I have a high art, I hurt with cruelty
those who would damage me.

Archilocus

Being vulnerable doesn't have to be
threatening.

Just have the courage to be sincere,
open and honest.

This opens the door to deeper
communication all around.

It creates self-empowerment and the
kind of connections with others we all
want in life.

Speaking from the heart frees us
from the secrets that burden us.

These secrets are what make us sick
or fearful.

Speaking truth helps you get clarity
on your real heart directives

Sara Paddison

Given enough time, any man may
master the physical.

With enough knowledge, any man
may become wise.

It is the true warrior who can master
both....and surpass the result.

Tien T'ai

Act like a man of thought.

Think like a man of action.

Thomas Mann

It is a brave act of valour to condemn
death, but where life is more terrible
than death it is then the truest valour
to dare to live.

Sir Thomas Brown

Your work is to discover your work
and then with all your heart to give
yourself to it.

Buddha

One mind, any weapon.

Hunter B. Armstrong

Civilise the mind but make savage the body.

Chairman Mao

Unless you do your best, the day will come when, tired and hungry, you will halt just short of the goal you were ordered to reach, and, by halting, you will make useless the efforts and deaths of thousands.

Gen. George S. Patton

I seek not only to follow in the
footsteps of the men of old, I seek
the things they sought

Basho

That which doesn't kill me, will make
me stronger!

Nietzche

We do not rise to the level of our expectations.

We fall to the level of our training.

Archilochus

Fear is the true opiate of combat

Budo Maxim

You must concentrate upon and consecrate yourself wholly to each day, as though a fire were raging in your hair.

Taisen Deshimaru

The test of a good teacher is not how
many questions he can ask his pupils
that they will answer readily, but how
many questions he inspires them to
ask him which he finds it hard to
answer.

Alice Wellington Rollins

In Germany, they came first for the Communists, and I didn't speak up because I wasn't a Communist.

Then they came for the Jews, and I didn't speak up because I wasn't a Jew.

Then they came for the trade unionists, and I didn't speak up because I wasn't a trade unionist.

Then they came for the Catholics, and I didn't speak up because I was Protestant.

Then they came for me, and by that time there was no one left to speak up.

Martin Niemoeller

Some Warriors look fierce, but are mild.

Some seem timid, but are vicious.

Look beyond appearances; position yourself for the advantage.

Deng Ming-Dao

Only a warrior chooses pacifism;
others are condemned to it.

Ueshiba

I dislike death, however, there are some things I dislike more than death.

Therefore, there are times when I will not avoid danger.

Mencius

Victory is reserved for those who are
willing to pay the price.

Sun Tzu

It does not matter how slowly you go
so long as you do not stop.

Confucius

War is not about who is right, it is about who is left

Bertrand Russell

All that we are is the result of what we have thought.

The mind is everything.

What we think we become.

Buddha

Only one who devotes himself to a
cause with his whole body and soul
can be a true master.

For this reason, mastery demands all
of a person

Albert Einstein

Talk is easy - ACTION is difficult.

Action is easy - TRUE
UNDERSTANDING is difficult!

Samurai Maxim

One finds life through conquering the
fear of death within one's mind.

Empty the mind of all forms of
attachment, make a go-for-broke
charge and conquer the opponent
with one decisive slash.

Togo Shigekata

The undisturbed mind is like the calm
body water reflecting the brilliance of
the moon.

Empty the mind and you will realise
the undisturbed mind.

Yagyu Jubei

You might as well stand and fight because if you run, you will only die tired.

Vern Jocque - Sei Shin Kan.

Each Warrior wants to leave the mark
of his will, his signature, on
important acts he touches.

This is not the voice of ego but of the
human spirit, rising up and declaring
that it has something to contribute to
the solution of the hardest problems,
no matter how vexing!

Pat Riley

When the world is at peace, a gentleman keeps his sword by his side.

Wu Tsu

Master the divine techniques of the
Art of Peace and no enemy will dare
to challenge you.

Ueshiba

In the beginners mind there are
many possibilities, but in the expert's
mind there are few.

Suzuki

To practice Zen or the Martial Arts,
you must live intensely,
wholeheartedly, without reserve - as
if you might die in the next instant.

Taisen Deshimaru

The Ultimate Warrior leaves no
openings; except in his mind.

Seishinkan

When the Way comes to an end, then
change - having changed, you pass
through.

I Ching

The more you sweat in training, the less you will bleed in battle.

Motto of US Navy Seals

The Way lies at hand yet it is sought
afar off; the thing lies in the easy yet
it is sought in the difficult.

Mencius

To think, *"I will not think"*

This, too, is something in one's thoughts.

Simply do not think about not thinking at all.

Takuan

The dance of battle is always played
to the same impatient rhythm.

What begins in a surge of violent
motion is always reduced to the
perfectly still.

Sun Tzu

At the end of your life, you will never regret not having passed one more test, not winning one more verdict, or not closing one more deal.

You will regret time not spent with a husband, a friend, a child, or a parent

Barbara Bush

SHUCHU RYOKU - Focus all your
energy to one point.

Shioda Gozo

Ultimately, you must forget about technique.

The further you progress, the fewer teachings there are.

The Great Path is really NO PATH.

Ueshiba Morihei

When you aim for perfection, you
discover it's a moving target.

Unknown

The no-mind not-thinks no-thoughts
about no-things.

Buddha

Victory goes to the one who has no
thought of himself.

**Shinkage School of
Swordsmanship**

Never give up on something that you can't go a day without thinking about.

Unknown

Be more concerned with your
character than your reputation,
because your character is what you
really are, while your reputation is
merely what others think you are.

John Wooden

In the world there is nothing more
submissive and weak than water.

Yet for attacking that which is hard
and strong nothing can surpass it.

Lao Tzu

See first with your mind, then with your eyes, and finally with your body

Yagyu Munenori

Teachers open the door, but you
must enter by yourself.

Chinese Proverb

Be master OF mind rather than
mastered BY mind.

Zen Saying

He who knows when he can fight and
when he cannot, will be victorious.

Sun Tzu

Good people do not need laws to tell them to act responsibly, while bad people will find a way around the laws.

Plato

If ignorant both of your enemy and yourself, you are certain to be in peril.

Sun Tzu

To understand the heart and mind of a person, look not at what he has already achieved, but at what he aspires to.

Kahlil Gibran

Never walk away from failure,
on the contrary, study it carefully,
and imaginatively for the hidden
assets.

Ian Finlayson

Those who are possessed by nothing
possess everything.

Morihei Ueshiba

Strategy without tactics is the
slowest route to victory.

Tactics without strategy is the noise
before defeat.

Sun Tzu

I'll moider da bum.

Heavyweight boxer Tony Galento, when asked what he thought of William Shakespeare

Excerpts From The Collected Sayings of Motobu Choki by

Marukawa Kenji

1. Everything is natural and changing.
2. Kamae is in the heart, not a physical manifestation.
3. One must develop the ability to read how much striking power someone has at a glance.
4. One does not have to take care to block every single attack by an opponent with weak striking power.
5. In a real confrontation, more than anything else, one should strike to the face first, as this is the most effective.
6. Kicks are not all that effective in a real confrontation.
7. Karate is sente (first strike).
8. The position of the legs and hips in Naifuanchin No Kata is the basics of karate.
9. Twisting to the left or to the right from Naifuanchin stance will give you the stance used in a real confrontation. Twisting one's way of thinking about Naifuanchin left and right, the various meanings in each of movement of the kata will become clear.
10. One must always try and block an attack at the source.
11. The blocking hand must be able to become the attacking hand in an instant. Blocking with one hand and then attacking with the other is not true bujutsu. Real bujutsu presses forward and blocks and counters in the same motion.
12. One cannot use continuous attacks against true karate. That is because the blocks of true karate make it impossible for the opponent to launch a second attack.
13. I still do not yet know the best way to punch the makiwara.
14. It's interesting, but when I just think about performing a kata, when I'm seated, I break a sweat.
15. When punching to the face, one must thrust as if punching through to the back of the head.
16. When fighting a boxer, it is better to go with his flow, and take up a rhythm with both of your hands.

293

17. **It is necessary to drink alcohol and pursue other fun human activities. The art of someone who is too serious has no flavour.**

18. It is okay to take two steps forward or backward in the same kamae, but over three steps, one must change the position of their guard.

19. When I fought the foreign boxer in Kyoto, he was taller than me so I jumped up and punched him in the face. This is effective against people who are taller than you.

20. I started having real fights at Tsuji when I was young, and fought over 100 of them, but I was never hit in the face.

21. When I was four, I was made to go to a school, but I hated studying, so I often skipped class and played somewhere with my friends.

22. When I was still in Okinawa, Kano Jigoro of the Kodokan visited and asked to talk with me, and through a friend we went to a certain restaurant. Mr. Kano talked about a lot of things, but about karate, he asked me what I would do if my punch missed. I answered that I would immediately follow with an elbow strike from that motion. After that, he became very quiet and asked nothing more about karate.

23. There are no stances such as neko-ashi, zenkutsu or kokutsu in my karate. Neko-ashi is a form of "floating foot" which is considered very bad in bujutsu. If one receives a body strike, one will be thrown off balance. Zenkutsu and kokutsu are unnatural, and prevent free leg movement.

24. The stance in my karate, whether in kata or kumite, is like Naifuanchin, with the knees slightly bent and the footwork is free. When defending or attacking, I tighten my knees and drop the hips, but I do not put my weight on either the front or the back foot, rather keeping it evenly distributed.

25. When blocking kicks, one must block as if trying to break the shin.

Funakoshi's Precepts

1. Karate-do begins with courtesy and ends with rei.

2. There is no first strike in karate.

3. Karate is an aid to justice.

4. First know yourself before attempting to know others.

5. Spirit first, technique second.

6. Always be ready to release your mind.

7. Accidents arise from negligence.

8. Do not think that karate training is only in the dojo.

9. It will take your entire life to learn karate, there is no limit.

10. Put your everyday living into karate and you will find "Myo" (subtle secrets).

11. Karate is like boiling water, if you do not heat it constantly, it will cool.

12. Do not think that you have to win, think rather that you do not have to lose.

13. Victory depends on your ability to distinguish vulnerable points from invulnerable ones.

14. The out come of the battle depends on how you handle weakness and strength.

15. Think of your opponents hands and feet as swords.

16. When you leave home, think that you have numerous opponents waiting for you.

17. Beginners must master low stance and posture; natural body positions are for the advanced.

18. Practicing a kata exactly is one thing, engaging in a real fight is another.

19. Do not forget to correctly apply: strength and weakness of power, stretching and contraction of the body, and slowness and speed of techniques.

20. Always think and devise ways to live the precepts of karate-do every day.

Do not get into a fight if you can possibly avoid it, but never hit soft.

Don't ever hit a man unless you must, but if you hit him, put him to sleep.

Theodore Roosevelt

Being deeply loved by someone gives you strength; loving someone deeply gives you courage.

Lao-Tzu

In the end, we will remember not the words of our enemies, but the silence of our friends.

Martin Luther King Jr

If you are far from the enemy, make
him believe you are near.

Sun Tzu

The only way to get rid of a
temptation is to yield to it.

Oscar Wilde

Nothing in the world is more
dangerous than sincere ignorance
and conscientious stupidity.

Martin Luther King, Jr

Try to learn something about
everything and everything about
something.

Thomas Henry Huxley

The only difference between me and
a madman is that I'm not mad.

Salvador Dali

Whenever I climb I am followed by a dog called 'Ego'.

Friedrich Nietzsche

Everybody pities the weak.

Jealousy you have to earn.

Arnold Schwarzenegger

Look at every path closely and
deliberately, then ask ourselves this
crucial question:

Does this path have a heart?

If it does, then the path is good.

If it doesn't, it is of no use

Carlos Castaneda

The difference between 'involvement'
and 'commitment' is like an eggs-
and-ham breakfast: the chicken was
'involved' - the pig was 'committed

Brian Billick

If you are going through hell, keep going.

Sir Winston Churchill

When you do the common things in
life in an uncommon way, you will
command the attention of the world.

George Washington Carver

The self-confidence of the warrior is
not the self-confidence of the
average man.

The average man seeks certainty in
the eyes of the onlooker and calls
that self-confidence.

The warrior seeks impeccability in his
own eyes and calls that humbleness.

The average man is hooked to his
fellow men, while the warrior is
hooked only to infinity.

Carlos Castaneda

Once you eliminate the impossible,
whatever remains, no matter how
improbable, must be the truth.

Sherlock Holmes

The true measure of a man is how he treats someone who can do him absolutely no good.

Samuel Johnson

If you want to make an apple pie
from scratch, you must first create
the universe.

Carl Sagan

Knowledge speaks, but wisdom
listens.

Jimi Hendrix

I have often regretted my speech,
never my silence.

Xenocrates

If everything seems under control,
you're just not going fast enough.

Mario Andretti

There are people in the world so
hungry, that God cannot appear to
them except in the form of bread.

Gandhi

When you gaze long into the abyss,
the abyss also gazes into you.

Friedrich Nietzsche

The instinct of nearly all societies is
to lock up anybody who is truly free.

First, society begins by trying to beat
you up.

If this fails, they try to poison you.

If this fails too, they finish by
loading honours on your head.

Jean Cocteau

Success usually comes to those who
are too busy to be looking for it.

Henry David Thoreau

To be a warrior is not a simple matter
of wishing to be one.

It is rather an endless struggle that
will go on to the very last moment of
our lives.

Nobody is born a warrior, in exactly
the same way that nobody is born an
average man.

We make ourselves into one or the
other.

Carlos Castenada

Fill what's empty.

Empty what's full.

Scratch where it itches.

The Duchess of Windsor (when asked what is the secret of a long and happy life)

The secret of success is to know
something nobody else knows.

Aristotle Onassis

Everything has been figured out,
except how to live.

Jean-Paul Sartre

I challenge you to make your life a
masterpiece.

I challenge you to join the ranks of
those people who live what they
teach, who walk their talk.

Anthony Robbins

Well-timed silence hath more
eloquence than speech.

Martin Farquhar Tupper

I am not young enough to know
everything.

Oscar Wilde

When choosing between two evils, I always like to try the one I've never tried before.

Mae West

Where do you begin?

Perfect is a good place to start.

We must always focus on improving
things that are already perfect.

J. Viol

I don't want to achieve immortality
through my work; I want to achieve
immortality through not dying.

Woody Allen

Opportunities multiply as they are seized.

Sun Tzu

The best way to predict the future is
to invent it.

Alan Kay

Sometimes it is not enough to do our best; we must do what is required.

Sir Winston Churchill

Pretend inferiority and encourage his arrogance.

Sun Tzu

The man who goes alone can start today; but he who travels with another must wait till that other is ready.

Henry David Thoreau

A pessimist sees the difficulty in
every opportunity.

An optimist sees the opportunity in
every difficulty.

Sir Winston Churchill

I think it would be a good idea.

Mahatma Gandhi when asked what he thought of Western civilization

The only thing necessary for the triumph of evil is for good men to do nothing.

Edmund Burke

The backbone of surprise is fusing
speed with secrecy.

von Clausewitz

The right to swing my fist ends where the other man's nose begins.

Oliver Wendell Holmes

Lakota Instructions for Living

Friend do it this way - that is,
whatever you do in life,
do the very best you can
with both your heart and mind.

And if you do it that way,
the Power Of The Universe
will come to your assistance,
if your heart and mind are in Unity.

When one sits in the Hoop Of The
People,
one must be responsible because
All of Creation is related.
And the hurt of one is the hurt of all.
And the honour of one is the honour
of all.
And whatever we do effects
everything in the universe.

If you do it that way - that is,
if you truly join your heart and mind
as One - whatever you ask for,
that's the Way It's Going To Be.

**passed down from White Buffalo
Calf Woman**

Whatever is begun in anger ends in shame.

Benjamin Franklin

Out of suffering have emerged the
strongest souls.

The most massive characters are
seared with scars.

Kahlil Gibran

Every normal man must be tempted
at times to spit upon his hands, hoist
the black flag, and begin slitting
throats.

Henry Louis Mencken

Hold on to what is good; even if it's a
handful of earth.

Hold on to what you believe; even if
it's a tree that stands by itself.

Hold on to what you must do; even if
it's a long way from here.

Hold on to your life; even if it's
easier to let go.

Hold on to my hand; even if someday
I'll be gone away from you.

Pueblo Indian Prayer

Now, my good man, this is no time
for making enemies.

**Voltaire on his deathbed in
response to a priest asking that
he renounce Satan**

We are not retreating - we are
advancing in another direction.

General Douglas MacArthur

I choose a block of marble and chop
off whatever I don't need.

**Francois-Auguste Rodin when
asked how he managed to make
his remarkable statues**

Research is what I'm doing when I
don't know what I'm doing.

Wernher Von Braun

There are only two tragedies in life.

One is not getting what one wants,
and the other is getting it.

Oscar Wilde

Treat the Earth well.

It was not given to you by your parents.

It was loaned to you by your children.

We do not inherit the Earth from our ancestors.

We borrow it from our children.

Ancient Indian Proverb

There are only two ways to live your life.

One is as though nothing is a miracle.

The other is as though everything is a miracle.

Albert Einstein

So live your life that the fear of death can
never enter your heart.
Trouble no one about their religion;
respect others in their view, and demand
that they respect yours.
Love your life, perfect your life, beautify all
things in your life.

Seek to make your life long and its purpose
in the service of your people.
Prepare a noble death song for the day when
you go over the great divide.
Always give a word or a sign of salute when
meeting or passing a friend,
even a stranger, when in a lonely place.
Show respect to all people and grovel to
none.

When you arise in the morning give thanks
for the food and for the joy of living.
If you see no reason for giving thanks, the
fault lies only in yourself.

Abuse no one and no thing, for abuse turns
the wise ones to fools
and robs the spirit of its vision.

When it comes your time to die, be not like
those whose hearts are filled
with the fear of death, so that when their
time comes they weep
and pray for a little more time to live their
lives over again in a different way.

Sing your death song and die like a hero
going home.

**Chief Tecumseh (Crouching Tiger)
Shawnee Nation**

Four things that come not back:

The spoken word

The sped arrow

The past life

The neglected opportunity

Omar al Khattab

Just do it!

Nike
(probably the most successful
advertising motto in history)

Generosity is giving more than you can, and pride is taking less than you need.

Kahlil Gibran

If you know the enemy and know
yourself you need not fear the results
of a hundred battles.

Know thy self.

Know thine enemy.

A thousand battles.

A thousand victories.

Sun Tzu

You are the bows from which your children as living arrows are sent forth.

Kahlil Gibran

Nothing ever becomes real 'til it is experienced.

John Keats

Life is too short to be living
somebody else's dream.

Hugh Hefner

When all the trees have been cut
down,
when all the animals have been
hunted,
when all the waters are polluted,
when all the air is unsafe to breathe,
only then will you discover you
cannot eat money.

Cree Prophecy

You take your life in your own
hands, and what happens?

A terrible thing.

No-one to blame.

Erica Jong

The first spiritual law of success is
the law of pure potentiality.

This law is based on the fact that we
are, in our essential state, pure
consciousness.

Pure consciousness is pure
potentiality; it is the field of all
possibilities and infinite creativity.

Pure consciousness is our spiritual
essence.

Being infinite and unbounded, it is
also pure joy.

Other attributes of consciousness are
pure knowledge, infinite silence,
perfect balance, invincibility,
simplicity and bliss.

This is our essential nature.

Our essential nature is one of pure
potentiality.

Deepak Chopra

Be the change that you want to see
in the world.

Mohandas Gandhi

The American businessman was at the pier of a small coastal Mexican village when a small boat with just one fisherman docked. Inside the small boat were several large yellowfin tuna. The American complimented the Mexican on the quality of his fish and asked how long it took to catch them.

The Mexican replied, "Only a little while."
The American then asked why didn't he stay out longer and catch more fish. The Mexican said he had enough to support his family's immediate needs.

The American then asked, "But what do you do with the rest of your time?"

The Mexican fisherman said, "I sleep late, fish a little, play with my children, take siesta with my wife, Maria, and stroll into the village each evening where I sip wine and play guitar with my amigos. I have a full and busy life, señor."

The American scoffed, "I am a Harvard MBA and could help you. You should spend more time fishing and with the proceeds buy a bigger boat. With the proceeds from the bigger boat you could buy several boats and eventually you would have a fleet of fishing boats. Instead of selling your catch to a middleman you would sell directly to the processor, eventually opening your own cannery. You would control the product, processing and distribution. You would need to leave this small coastal fishing village and move to Mexico City, then Los Angeles, and eventually New York where you will run your expanding enterprise."

The Mexican fisherman asked, "But señor, how long will this all take?"

To which the American replied, "Fifteen to 20 years."

"But what then, señor?"
The American laughed and said, "That's the best part. When the time is right you would announce an IPO and sell your companies stock to the public and become very rich. You would make millions."

"Millions, señor? Then what?"
The American said, "Then you would retire. Move to a small coastal fishing village where you would sleep late, fish a little, play with your kids, take siesta with your wife, stroll to the village in the evenings where you could sip wine and play your guitar with your amigos."

366

We learn wisdom from failure much
more than from success.

We often discover what will do, by
finding out what will not do; and
probably he who never made a
mistake never made a discovery.

Samuel Smiles

In the end, it's not going to matter how many breaths you took, but how many moments took your breath away.

Shing Xiong

The following is an actual question given on a University of Washington engineering mid-term. The answer was so "profound" that the Professor shared it with colleagues..

Bonus Question: Is Hell exothermic (gives off heat) or Endothermic (absorbs heat)?

Most of the students wrote Proofs of their beliefs using Boyle's Law, (gas cools off when it expands and heats when it is compressed) or some variant. One student, however, wrote the following:

"First, we need to know how the mass of Hell is changing in time. So we need to know the rate that souls are moving into Hell and the rate they are leaving. I think that we can safely assume that once a soul gets to Hell, it will not leave. Therefore, no souls are leaving. As for how many souls are entering Hell, let us look at the different religions that exist in the world today. Some of these religions state that if you are not a member of their religion, you will go to Hell. Since there are more than one of these religions and since people do not belong to more than one religion, we can project that all souls go to Hell. With birth and death rates as they are, we can expect the number of souls in Hell to increase exponentially.

Now, we look at the rate of change of the volume in Hell because Boyle's Law states that in order for the temperature and pressure in Hell to stay the same, the volume of Hell has to expand as souls are added. This gives two possibilities:

1. If Hell is expanding at a slower rate than the rate at which souls enter Hell, then the temperature and pressure in Hell will increase until all Hell breaks loose.

2. Of course, if Hell is expanding at a rate faster than the increase of souls in Hell, then the temperature and pressure will drop until Hell freezes over.

So which is it?

If we accept the postulate given to me by Teresa Banyan during my Freshman year, "...that it will be a cold day in Hell before I sleep with you.", and take into account the fact that I still have not succeeded in having sexual relations with her, then, #2 cannot be true, and thus I am sure that Hell is exothermic and will not freeze."

This student received the only A.

Work like you don't need the money,
love like you've never been hurt and
dance like no one is watching.

Randall G Leighton

A mother passing by her daughter's bedroom was astonished to see the bed was nicely made and everything was picked up. Then she saw an envelope propped up prominently on the center of the bed. It was addressed, "Mom." With the worst premonition, she opened the envelope and read the letter with trembling hands:

Dear Mom: It is with great regret and sorrow that I'm writing you. I had to elope with my new boyfriend because I wanted to avoid a scene with Dad and you. I've been finding real passion with Ahmed and he is so nice- even with all his piercings, tattoos, beard, and his motorcycle clothes. But it's not only the passion Mom, I'm pregnant and Ahmed said that we will be very happy. He already owns a trailer in the woods and has a stack of firewood for the whole winter. He wants to have many more children with me and that's now one of my dreams too. Ahmed taught me that marijuana doesn't really hurt anyone and we'll be growing it for us and trading it with his friends for all the cocaine and ecstasy we want. In the meantime, we'll pray that science will find a cure for AIDS so Ahmed can get better; he sure deserves it!! Don't worry Mom, I'm 15 years old now and I know how to take care of myself. Someday I'm sure we'll be back to visit so you can get to know your grand children.

Your daughter, Judith

PS: Mom, none of the above is true. I'm over at the neighbour's house. I just wanted to remind you that there are worse things in life than my report card that's in my desk drawer. I love you! Call when it is safe for me to come home.

The softest things in the world
overcome the hardest things in the
world.

Lao Tzu

If you love somebody, let them go, for
if they return, they were always yours.

And if they don't, they never were.

Kahlil Gibran

Advice is what we ask for when we already know the answer but wish we didn't.

Erica Jong

When I die, I want to die like my grandmother, who died peacefully in her sleep.

Not screaming like all the passengers in her car.

Amen